Reading Log Book

This Journal belongs to :

_____

Nr	Book Title	Author's name	Rating
1			☆☆☆☆☆
2			☆☆☆☆☆
3			☆☆☆☆☆
4			☆☆☆☆☆
5			☆☆☆☆☆
6			☆☆☆☆☆
7			☆☆☆☆☆
8			☆☆☆☆☆
9			☆☆☆☆☆
10			☆☆☆☆☆
11			☆☆☆☆☆
12			☆☆☆☆☆
13			☆☆☆☆☆
14			☆☆☆☆☆
15			☆☆☆☆☆
16			☆☆☆☆☆
17			☆☆☆☆☆
18			☆☆☆☆☆
19			☆☆☆☆☆
20			☆☆☆☆☆
21			☆☆☆☆☆
22			☆☆☆☆☆
23			☆☆☆☆☆
24			☆☆☆☆☆
25			☆☆☆☆☆

Nr	Book Title	Author's name	Rating
26			☆☆☆☆☆
27			☆☆☆☆☆
28			☆☆☆☆☆
29			☆☆☆☆☆
30			☆☆☆☆☆
31			☆☆☆☆☆
32			☆☆☆☆☆
33			☆☆☆☆☆
34			☆☆☆☆☆
35			☆☆☆☆☆
36			☆☆☆☆☆
37			☆☆☆☆☆
38			☆☆☆☆☆
39			☆☆☆☆☆
40			☆☆☆☆☆
41			☆☆☆☆☆
42			☆☆☆☆☆
43			☆☆☆☆☆
44			☆☆☆☆☆
45			☆☆☆☆☆
46			☆☆☆☆☆
47			☆☆☆☆☆
48			☆☆☆☆☆
49			☆☆☆☆☆
50			☆☆☆☆☆

Nr	Book Title	Author's name	Rating
51			☆☆☆☆☆
52			☆☆☆☆☆
53			☆☆☆☆☆
54			☆☆☆☆☆
55			☆☆☆☆☆
56			☆☆☆☆☆
57			☆☆☆☆☆
58			☆☆☆☆☆
59			☆☆☆☆☆
60			☆☆☆☆☆
61			☆☆☆☆☆
62			☆☆☆☆☆
63			☆☆☆☆☆
64			☆☆☆☆☆
65			☆☆☆☆☆
66			☆☆☆☆☆
67			☆☆☆☆☆
68			☆☆☆☆☆
69			☆☆☆☆☆
70			☆☆☆☆☆
71			☆☆☆☆☆
72			☆☆☆☆☆
73			☆☆☆☆☆
74			☆☆☆☆☆
75			☆☆☆☆☆

Nr	Book Title	Author's name	Rating
76			☆☆☆☆☆
77			☆☆☆☆☆
78			☆☆☆☆☆
79			☆☆☆☆☆
80			☆☆☆☆☆
81			☆☆☆☆☆
82			☆☆☆☆☆
83			☆☆☆☆☆
84			☆☆☆☆☆
85			☆☆☆☆☆
86			☆☆☆☆☆
87			☆☆☆☆☆
88			☆☆☆☆☆
89			☆☆☆☆☆
90			☆☆☆☆☆
91			☆☆☆☆☆
92			☆☆☆☆☆
93			☆☆☆☆☆
94			☆☆☆☆☆
95			☆☆☆☆☆
96			☆☆☆☆☆
97			☆☆☆☆☆
98			☆☆☆☆☆
99			☆☆☆☆☆
100			☆☆☆☆☆

Book Title:_____

Author:_____

Summary:

Favorite Character: _____

Best part of the book:

Favorite Quotes:

Would you recommend this book to a friend: YES / NO

Rating

☆ ☆ ☆ ☆ ☆

1

Book Title:_____

Author:_____

Summary:

Favorite Character: _____

Best part of the book:

Favorite Quotes:

Would you recommend this book to a friend: YES / NO

Rating

☆ ☆ ☆ ☆ ☆

2

Book Title:_____

Author:_____

Summary:

Favorite Character: _____

Best part of the book:

Favorite Quotes:

Would you recommend this book to a friend: YES / NO

Rating

3

Book Title:_____

Author:_____

Summary:

Favorite Character: _____

Best part of the book:

Favorite Quotes:

Would you recommend this book to a friend: YES / NO

Rating

☆ ☆ ☆ ☆ ☆

4

Book Title:_____

Author:_____

Summary:

Favorite Character: _____

Best part of the book:

Favorite Quotes:

Would you recommend this book to a friend: YES / NO

Rating

☆ ☆ ☆ ☆ ☆   5

Book Title:_____

Author:_____

Summary:

Favorite Character: _____

Best part of the book:

Favorite Quotes:

Would you recommend this book to a friend: YES / NO

Rating

☆ ☆ ☆ ☆ ☆

6

Book Title:_____

Author:_____

Summary:

Favorite Character: _____

Best part of the book:

Favorite Quotes:

Would you recommend this book to a friend: YES / NO

Rating
☆ ☆ ☆ ☆ ☆

Book Title:_____

Author:_____

Summary:

Favorite Character: _____

Best part of the book:

Favorite Quotes:

Would you recommend this book to a friend: YES / NO

Rating

☆ ☆ ☆ ☆ ☆

Book Title:_____

Author:_____

Summary:

Favorite Character: _____

Best part of the book:

Favorite Quotes:

Would you recommend this book to a friend: YES / NO

Rating
☆ ☆ ☆ ☆ ☆

Book Title:_____

Author:_____

Summary:

Favorite Character: _____

Best part of the book:

Favorite Quotes:

Would you recommend this book to a friend: YES / NO

Rating

☆ ☆ ☆ ☆ ☆

10

Book Title:_____

Author:_____

Summary:

Favorite Character: _____

Best part of the book:

Favorite Quotes:

Would you recommend this book to a friend: YES / NO

Rating

11

Book Title:_____

Author:_____

Summary:

Favorite Character: _____

Best part of the book:

Favorite Quotes:

Would you recommend this book to a friend: YES / NO

Rating

☆ ☆ ☆ ☆ ☆

12

Book Title:_____

Author:_____

Summary:

Favorite Character: _____

Best part of the book:

Favorite Quotes:

Would you recommend this book to a friend: YES / NO

Rating

☆ ☆ ☆ ☆ ☆

13

Book Title:_____

Author:_____

Summary:

Favorite Character: _____

Best part of the book:

Favorite Quotes:

Would you recommend this book to a friend: YES / NO

Rating

☆ ☆ ☆ ☆ ☆

14

Book Title:_____

Author:_____

Summary:

Favorite Character: _____

Best part of the book:

Favorite Quotes:

Would you recommend this book to a friend: YES / NO

Rating

15

Book Title:_____

Author:_____

Summary:

Favorite Character: _____

Best part of the book:

Favorite Quotes:

Would you recommend this book to a friend: YES / NO

Rating

☆ ☆ ☆ ☆ ☆

Book Title:_____

Author:_____

Summary:

Favorite Character: _____

Best part of the book:

Favorite Quotes:

Would you recommend this book to a friend: YES / NO

Rating
☆ ☆ ☆ ☆ ☆

Book Title:_____

Author:_____

Summary:

Favorite Character: _____

Best part of the book:

Favorite Quotes:

Would you recommend this book to a friend: YES / NO

Rating

☆ ☆ ☆ ☆ ☆

18

Book Title:_____

Author:_____

Summary:

Favorite Character: _____

Best part of the book:

Favorite Quotes:

Would you recommend this book to a friend: YES / NO

Rating

☆ ☆ ☆ ☆ ☆

19

Book Title:_____

Author:_____

Summary:

Favorite Character: _____

Best part of the book:

Favorite Quotes:

Would you recommend this book to a friend: YES / NO

Rating
☆ ☆ ☆ ☆ ☆

20

Book Title:_____

Author:_____

Summary:

Favorite Character: _____

Best part of the book:

Favorite Quotes:

Would you recommend this book to a friend: YES / NO

Rating
☆ ☆ ☆ ☆ ☆

Book Title:_____

Author:_____

Summary:

Favorite Character: _____

Best part of the book:

Favorite Quotes:

Would you recommend this book to a friend: YES / NO

Rating

☆ ☆ ☆ ☆ ☆

22

Book Title:_____

Author:_____

Summary:

Favorite Character: _____

Best part of the book:

Favorite Quotes:

Would you recommend this book to a friend: YES / NO

Rating

23

Book Title:_____

Author:_____

Summary:

Favorite Character: _____

Best part of the book:

Favorite Quotes:

Would you recommend this book to a friend: YES / NO

Rating

☆ ☆ ☆ ☆ ☆

24

Book Title:_____

Author:_____

Summary:

Favorite Character: _____

Best part of the book:

Favorite Quotes:

Would you recommend this book to a friend: YES / NO

Rating
☆ ☆ ☆ ☆ ☆

25

Book Title:_____

Author:_____

Summary:

Favorite Character: _____

Best part of the book:

Favorite Quotes:

Would you recommend this book to a friend: YES / NO

Rating

☆ ☆ ☆ ☆ ☆

26

Book Title:_____

Author:_____

Summary:

Favorite Character: _____

Best part of the book:

Favorite Quotes:

Would you recommend this book to a friend: YES / NO

Rating

☆ ☆ ☆ ☆ ☆

27

Book Title:_____

Author:_____

Summary:

Favorite Character: _____

Best part of the book:

Favorite Quotes:

Would you recommend this book to a friend: YES / NO

Rating

☆ ☆ ☆ ☆ ☆

28

Book Title:_____

Author:_____

Summary:

Favorite Character: _____

Best part of the book:

Favorite Quotes:

Would you recommend this book to a friend: YES / NO

Rating

☆ ☆ ☆ ☆ ☆

29

Book Title:_____

Author:_____

Summary:

Favorite Character: _____

Best part of the book:

Favorite Quotes:

Would you recommend this book to a friend: YES / NO

Rating

Book Title:_____

Author:_____

Summary:

Favorite Character: _____

Best part of the book:

Favorite Quotes:

Would you recommend this book to a friend: YES / NO

Rating
☆ ☆ ☆ ☆ ☆

31

Book Title:_____

Author:_____

Summary:

Favorite Character: _____

Best part of the book:

Favorite Quotes:

Would you recommend this book to a friend: YES / NO

Rating

☆ ☆ ☆ ☆ ☆

32

Book Title:_____

Author:_____

Summary:

Favorite Character: _____

Best part of the book:

Favorite Quotes:

Would you recommend this book to a friend: YES / NO

Rating

Book Title:_____

Author:_____

Summary:

Favorite Character: _____

Best part of the book:

Favorite Quotes:

Would you recommend this book to a friend: YES / NO

Rating

☆ ☆ ☆ ☆ ☆

Book Title:_____

Author:_____

Summary:

Favorite Character: _____

Best part of the book:

Favorite Quotes:

Would you recommend this book to a friend: YES / NO

Rating

☆ ☆ ☆ ☆ ☆

35

Book Title:_____

Author:_____

Summary:

Favorite Character: _____

Best part of the book:

Favorite Quotes:

Would you recommend this book to a friend: YES / NO

Rating

☆ ☆ ☆ ☆ ☆

36

Book Title:_____

Author:_____

Summary:

Favorite Character: _____

Best part of the book:

Favorite Quotes:

Would you recommend this book to a friend: YES / NO

Rating

37

Book Title:_____

Author:_____

Summary:

Favorite Character: _____

Best part of the book:

Favorite Quotes:

Would you recommend this book to a friend: YES / NO

Rating

☆ ☆ ☆ ☆ ☆

Book Title:_____

Author:_____

Summary:

Favorite Character: _____

Best part of the book:

Favorite Quotes:

Would you recommend this book to a friend: YES / NO

Rating

☆ ☆ ☆ ☆ ☆

39

Book Title:_____

Author:_____

Summary:

Favorite Character: _____

Best part of the book:

Favorite Quotes:

Would you recommend this book to a friend: YES / NO

Rating

☆ ☆ ☆ ☆ ☆

40

Book Title:_____

Author:_____

Summary:

Favorite Character: _____

Best part of the book:

Favorite Quotes:

Would you recommend this book to a friend: YES / NO

Rating

☆ ☆ ☆ ☆ ☆

Book Title:_____

Author:_____

Summary:

Favorite Character: _____

Best part of the book:

Favorite Quotes:

Would you recommend this book to a friend: YES / NO

Rating

☆ ☆ ☆ ☆ ☆

42

Book Title:_____

Author:_____

Summary:

Favorite Character: _____

Best part of the book:

Favorite Quotes:

Would you recommend this book to a friend: YES / NO

Rating

☆ ☆ ☆ ☆ ☆

43

Book Title:_____

Author:_____

Summary:

Favorite Character: _____

Best part of the book:

Favorite Quotes:

Would you recommend this book to a friend: YES / NO

Rating

☆ ☆ ☆ ☆ ☆

44

Book Title:_____

Author:_____

Summary:

Favorite Character: _____

Best part of the book:

Favorite Quotes:

Would you recommend this book to a friend: YES / NO

Rating

45

Book Title:_____

Author:_____

Summary:

Favorite Character: _____

Best part of the book:

Favorite Quotes:

Would you recommend this book to a friend: YES / NO

Rating
☆ ☆ ☆ ☆ ☆

46

Book Title:_____

Author:_____

Summary:

Favorite Character: _____

Best part of the book:

Favorite Quotes:

Would you recommend this book to a friend: YES / NO

Rating

☆ ☆ ☆ ☆ ☆

47

Book Title:_____

Author:_____

Summary:

Favorite Character: _____

Best part of the book:

Favorite Quotes:

Would you recommend this book to a friend: YES / NO

Rating

☆ ☆ ☆ ☆ ☆

48

Book Title:_____

Author:_____

Summary:

Favorite Character: _____

Best part of the book:

Favorite Quotes:

Would you recommend this book to a friend: YES / NO

Rating

☆ ☆ ☆ ☆ ☆

49

Book Title:_____

Author:_____

Summary:

Favorite Character: _____

Best part of the book:

Favorite Quotes:

Would you recommend this book to a friend: YES / NO

Rating

☆ ☆ ☆ ☆ ☆

50

Book Title:_____

Author:_____

Summary:

Favorite Character: _____

Best part of the book:

Favorite Quotes:

Would you recommend this book to a friend: YES / NO

Rating

51

Book Title:_____

Author:_____

Summary:

Favorite Character: _____

Best part of the book:

Favorite Quotes:

Would you recommend this book to a friend: YES / NO

Rating

52

Book Title:_____

Author:_____

Summary:

Favorite Character: _____

Best part of the book:

Favorite Quotes:

Would you recommend this book to a friend: YES / NO

Rating
☆ ☆ ☆ ☆ ☆

53

Book Title:_____

Author:_____

Summary:

Favorite Character: _____

Best part of the book:

Favorite Quotes:

Would you recommend this book to a friend: YES / NO

Rating

☆ ☆ ☆ ☆ ☆

54

Book Title:_____

Author:_____

Summary:

Favorite Character: _____

Best part of the book:

Favorite Quotes:

Would you recommend this book to a friend: YES / NO

Rating

55

Book Title:_____

Author:_____

Summary:

Favorite Character: _____

Best part of the book:

Favorite Quotes:

Would you recommend this book to a friend: YES / NO

Rating

☆ ☆ ☆ ☆ ☆

56

Book Title:_____

Author:_____

Summary:

Favorite Character: _____

Best part of the book:

Favorite Quotes:

Would you recommend this book to a friend: YES / NO

Rating

Book Title:_____

Author:_____

Summary:

Favorite Character: _____

Best part of the book:

Favorite Quotes:

Would you recommend this book to a friend: YES / NO

Rating

58

Book Title:_____

Author:_____

Summary:

Favorite Character: _____

Best part of the book:

Favorite Quotes:

Would you recommend this book to a friend: YES / NO

Rating

☆ ☆ ☆ ☆ ☆

59

Book Title:_____

Author:_____

Summary:

Favorite Character: _____

Best part of the book:

Favorite Quotes:

Would you recommend this book to a friend: YES / NO

Rating

☆ ☆ ☆ ☆ ☆

60

Book Title:_____

Author:_____

Summary:

Favorite Character: _____

Best part of the book:

Favorite Quotes:

Would you recommend this book to a friend: YES / NO

Rating

☆ ☆ ☆ ☆ ☆

Book Title:_____

Author:_____

Summary:

Favorite Character: _____

Best part of the book:

Favorite Quotes:

Would you recommend this book to a friend: YES / NO

Rating

☆ ☆ ☆ ☆ ☆

62

Book Title:_____

Author:_____

Summary:

Favorite Character: _____

Best part of the book:

Favorite Quotes:

Would you recommend this book to a friend: YES / NO

Rating

☆ ☆ ☆ ☆ ☆

63

Book Title:_____

Author:_____

Summary:

Favorite Character: _____

Best part of the book:

Favorite Quotes:

Would you recommend this book to a friend: YES / NO

Rating

64

Book Title:_____

Author:_____

Summary:

Favorite Character: _____

Best part of the book:

Favorite Quotes:

Would you recommend this book to a friend: YES / NO

Rating

☆ ☆ ☆ ☆ ☆

65

Book Title:_____

Author:_____

Summary:

Favorite Character: _____

Best part of the book:

Favorite Quotes:

Would you recommend this book to a friend: YES / NO

Rating

☆ ☆ ☆ ☆ ☆

66

Book Title:_____

Author:_____

Summary:

Favorite Character: _____

Best part of the book:

Favorite Quotes:

Would you recommend this book to a friend: YES / NO

Rating
☆ ☆ ☆ ☆ ☆

Book Title:_____

Author:_____

Summary:

Favorite Character: _____

Best part of the book:

Favorite Quotes:

Would you recommend this book to a friend: YES / NO

Rating

☆ ☆ ☆ ☆ ☆

68

Book Title:_____

Author:_____

Summary:

Favorite Character: _____

Best part of the book:

Favorite Quotes:

Would you recommend this book to a friend: YES / NO

Rating

69

Book Title:_____

Author:_____

Summary:

Favorite Character: _____

Best part of the book:

Favorite Quotes:

Would you recommend this book to a friend: YES / NO

Rating

☆ ☆ ☆ ☆ ☆

70

Book Title:_____

Author:_____

Summary:

Favorite Character: _____

Best part of the book:

Favorite Quotes:

Would you recommend this book to a friend: YES / NO

Rating

71

Book Title:_____

Author:_____

Summary:

Favorite Character: _____

Best part of the book:

Favorite Quotes:

Would you recommend this book to a friend: YES / NO

Rating

☆ ☆ ☆ ☆ ☆

72

Book Title:_____

Author:_____

Summary:

Favorite Character: _____

Best part of the book:

Favorite Quotes:

Would you recommend this book to a friend: YES / NO

Rating

☆ ☆ ☆ ☆ ☆

73

Book Title:_____

Author:_____

Summary:

Favorite Character: _____

Best part of the book:

Favorite Quotes:

Would you recommend this book to a friend: YES / NO

Rating

☆ ☆ ☆ ☆ ☆

74

Book Title:_____

Author:_____

Summary:

Favorite Character: _____

Best part of the book:

Favorite Quotes:

Would you recommend this book to a friend: YES / NO

Rating

☆ ☆ ☆ ☆ ☆

75

Book Title:_____

Author:_____

Summary:

Favorite Character: _____

Best part of the book:

Favorite Quotes:

Would you recommend this book to a friend: YES / NO

Rating

☆ ☆ ☆ ☆ ☆

76

Book Title:_____

Author:_____

Summary:

Favorite Character: _____

Best part of the book:

Favorite Quotes:

Would you recommend this book to a friend: YES / NO

Rating
☆ ☆ ☆ ☆ ☆

Book Title:_____

Author:_____

Summary:

Favorite Character: _____

Best part of the book:

Favorite Quotes:

Would you recommend this book to a friend: YES / NO

Rating

☆ ☆ ☆ ☆ ☆

78

Book Title: _____

Author: _____

Summary:

Favorite Character: _____

Best part of the book:

Favorite Quotes:

Would you recommend this book to a friend: YES / NO

Rating

79

Book Title:_____

Author:_____

Summary:

Favorite Character: _____

Best part of the book:

Favorite Quotes:

Would you recommend this book to a friend: YES / NO

Rating

☆ ☆ ☆ ☆ ☆

80

Book Title:_____

Author:_____

Summary:

Favorite Character: _____

Best part of the book:

Favorite Quotes:

Would you recommend this book to a friend: YES / NO

Rating
☆ ☆ ☆ ☆ ☆

Book Title:_____

Author:_____

Summary:

Favorite Character: _____

Best part of the book:

Favorite Quotes:

Would you recommend this book to a friend: YES / NO

Rating

82

Book Title:_____

Author:_____

Summary:

Favorite Character: _____

Best part of the book:

Favorite Quotes:

Would you recommend this book to a friend: YES / NO

Rating

☆ ☆ ☆ ☆ ☆

83

Book Title:_____

Author:_____

Summary:

Favorite Character: _____

Best part of the book:

Favorite Quotes:

Would you recommend this book to a friend: YES / NO

Rating

☆ ☆ ☆ ☆ ☆

84

Book Title:_____

Author:_____

Summary:

Favorite Character: _____

Best part of the book:

Favorite Quotes:

Would you recommend this book to a friend: YES / NO

Rating

85

Book Title:_____

Author:_____

Summary:

Favorite Character: _____

Best part of the book:

Favorite Quotes:

Would you recommend this book to a friend: YES / NO

Rating
☆ ☆ ☆ ☆ ☆

86

Book Title:_____

Author:_____

Summary:

Favorite Character: _____

Best part of the book:

Favorite Quotes:

Would you recommend this book to a friend: YES / NO

Rating

☆ ☆ ☆ ☆ ☆

Book Title:_____

Author:_____

Summary:

Favorite Character: _____

Best part of the book:

Favorite Quotes:

Would you recommend this book to a friend: YES / NO

Rating

☆ ☆ ☆ ☆ ☆

Book Title:_____

Author:_____

Summary:

Favorite Character: _____

Best part of the book:

Favorite Quotes:

Would you recommend this book to a friend: YES / NO

Rating

☆ ☆ ☆ ☆ ☆

89

Book Title:_____

Author:_____

Summary:

Favorite Character: _____

Best part of the book:

Favorite Quotes:

Would you recommend this book to a friend: YES / NO

Rating

☆ ☆ ☆ ☆ ☆

90

Book Title:_____

Author:_____

Summary:

Favorite Character: _____

Best part of the book:

Favorite Quotes:

Would you recommend this book to a friend: YES / NO

Rating

Book Title:_____

Author:_____

Summary:

Favorite Character: _____

Best part of the book:

Favorite Quotes:

Would you recommend this book to a friend: YES / NO

Rating

☆ ☆ ☆ ☆ ☆

92

Book Title:_____

Author:_____

Summary:

Favorite Character: _____

Best part of the book:

Favorite Quotes:

Would you recommend this book to a friend: YES / NO

Rating

93

Book Title:_____

Author:_____

Summary:

Favorite Character: _____

Best part of the book:

Favorite Quotes:

Would you recommend this book to a friend: YES / NO

Rating

☆ ☆ ☆ ☆ ☆

94

Book Title:_____

Author:_____

Summary:

Favorite Character: _____

Best part of the book:

Favorite Quotes:

Would you recommend this book to a friend: YES / NO

Rating

☆ ☆ ☆ ☆ ☆

95

Book Title:_____

Author:_____

Summary:

Favorite Character: _____

Best part of the book:

Favorite Quotes:

Would you recommend this book to a friend: YES / NO

Rating

96

Book Title:_____

Author:_____

Summary:

Favorite Character: _____

Best part of the book:

Favorite Quotes:

Would you recommend this book to a friend: YES / NO

Rating

☆ ☆ ☆ ☆ ☆

97

Book Title:_____

Author:_____

Summary:

Favorite Character: _____

Best part of the book:

Favorite Quotes:

Would you recommend this book to a friend: YES / NO

Rating

☆ ☆ ☆ ☆ ☆

98

Book Title:_____

Author:_____

Summary:

Favorite Character: _____

Best part of the book:

Favorite Quotes:

Would you recommend this book to a friend: YES / NO

Rating

☆ ☆ ☆ ☆ ☆

Book Title:_____

Author:_____

Summary:

Favorite Character: _____

Best part of the book:

Favorite Quotes:

Would you recommend this book to a friend: YES / NO

Rating

☆ ☆ ☆ ☆ ☆

100

CPSIA information can be obtained
at www.ICGtesting.com
Printed in the USA
LVHW051234130221
679242LV00023B/1611